THE BEATLES

Solos and Band Arrangements
Correlated with Essential Elements® Band Method

Arranged by
ROBERT LONGFIELD, JOHNNIE VINSON and JOHN MOSS

Welcome to ESSENTIAL ELE[...] [...]angements in this versatile book can be used either in a full co[...] [...]s for individual instruments. The SOLO pages appear at the be[...] [...] followed by the BAND ARRANGEMENT pages. The supplemental CD recording or PIANO ACCOMPANIMENT book may be used as an accompaniment for solo performance.

ISBN 978-1-4234-7636-8

HAL•LEONARD® CORPORATION
7777 W. BLUEMOUND RD. P.O. BOX 13819 MILWAUKEE, WI 53213

00860236

From A HARD DAY'S NIGHT

AND I LOVE HER

Words and Music by
JOHN LENNON and PAUL McCARTNEY
Arranged by JOHNNIE VINSON

00860236

From A HARD DAY'S NIGHT

A HARD DAY'S NIGHT

Words and Music by
JOHN LENNON and **PAUL McCARTNEY**
Arranged by JOHN MOSS

00860236

YESTERDAY

Words and Music by
JOHN LENNON and **PAUL McCARTNEY**
Arranged by JOHN MOSS

GET BACK

Words and Music by
JOHN LENNON and **PAUL McCARTNEY**
Arranged by JOHNNIE VINSON

LADY MADONNA

Words and Music by
JOHN LENNON and PAUL McCARTNEY
Arranged by ROBERT LONGFIELD

TWIST AND SHOUT

Words and Music by
BERT RUSSELL and PHIL MEDLEY
Arranged by ROBERT LONGFIELD

HEY JUDE

Words and Music by
JOHN LENNON and **PAUL McCARTNEY**
Arranged by ROBERT LONGFIELD

00860236

ELEANOR RIGBY

Words and Music by
JOHN LENNON and **PAUL McCARTNEY**
Arranged by ROBERT LONGFIELD

00860236

Featured in the Motion Picture HELP!

TICKET TO RIDE

Words and Music by
JOHN LENNON and **PAUL McCARTNEY**
Arranged by ROBERT LONGFIELD

28

HERE, THERE AND EVERYWHERE

Words and Music by
JOHN LENNON and **PAUL McCARTNEY**
Arranged by JOHNNIE VINSON

I WANT TO HOLD YOUR HAND

Words and Music by
JOHN LENNON and PAUL McCARTNEY
Arranged by JOHNNIE VINSON

00860236

MORE FAVORITES FROM ESSENTIAL ELEMENTS

Each song appears twice in the book, featuring:
- Solo instrument version
- Band arrangement for full band or ensembles
- Pop-style accompaniment CD included with conductor's score
- Accompaniment CD available separately
- Piano accompaniment book that is compatible with recorded backgrounds

Prices:
- Conductor Books $24.99
- Instrument Books $6.99
- Piano Accompaniment Books $11.99
- Accompaniment CDs. $12.99

Instrument books for each collection feature separate books for the following: Flute, Oboe, Bassoon, B♭ Clarinet, E♭ Alto Clarinet, B♭ Bass Clarinet, E♭ Alto Saxophone, B♭ Tenor Saxophone, E♭ Baritone Saxophone, B♭ Trumpet, F Horn, Trombone, Baritone B.C., Baritone T.C., Tuba, Percussion, and Keyboard Percussion.

These superb collections feature favorite songs that students can play as they progress through their band method books. Each song is arranged to be played by either a full band or by individual soloists, with optional accompaniment on CD.

BROADWAY FAVORITES
Arranged by Michael Sweeney
Songs include:
Beauty and the Beast
Tomorrow
Cabaret
Edelweiss
Don't Cry for Me Argentina
Get Me to the Church on Time
I Dreamed a Dream
Go Go Go Joseph
Memory
The Phantom of the Opera
Seventy Six Trombones

CHRISTMAS FAVORITES
Arranged by Michael Sweeney
Songs include:
The Christmas Song
  (Chestnuts Roasting on an Open Fire)
Frosty the Snow Man
A Holly Jolly Christmas
Jingle-Bell Rock
Let It Snow! Let It Snow! Let It Snow!
Rockin' Around the Christmas Tree
Rudolph, the Red-Nosed Reindeer.

FILM FAVORITES
Arranged by Michael Sweeney, John Moss and Paul Lavender
Songs include:
The Black Pearl
Fairytale Opening
Mission: Impossible Theme
My Heart Will Go On
Zorro's Theme
Music from Shrek
May It Be
The Medallion Calls
You'll Be in My Heart
The Rainbow Connection
Accidentally in Love
Also Sprach Zarathustra

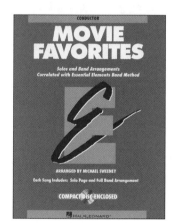

MOVIE FAVORITES
Arranged by Michael Sweeney
Includes themes from:
An American Tail
Back to the Future
Chariots of Fire
Apollo 13
E.T.
Forrest Gump
Dances with Wolves
Jurassic Park
The Man from Snowy River
Raiders of the Lost Ark
Star Trek

PATRIOTIC FAVORITES
Arranged by Michael Sweeney
Songs include:
America, the Beautiful
Armed Forces Salute
Battle Hymn of the Republic
God Bless America
Hymn to the Fallen
My Country, 'Tis of Thee (America)
The Patriot
The Star Spangled Banner
Stars and Stripes Forever
This Is My Country
Yankee Doodle/Yankee Dookle Boy

PERFORMANCE FAVORITES, VOL. 1
Arranged by Michael Sweeney, Paul Lavender, John Higgins, John Moss and James Curnow
Songs include:
African Sketches
Barrier Reef
Do You Hear What I Hear
Regimental Honor
Spinning Wheel
You're a Grand Old Flag
British Masters Suite
Elves' Dance
On Broadway
Summon the Heroes
Two Celtic Dances

FOR MORE INFORMATION, SEE YOUR LOCAL MUSIC DEALER, OR WRITE TO:

HAL•LEONARD® CORPORATION
7777 W. BLUEMOUND RD. P.O. BOX 13819 MILWAUKEE, WI 53213

Visit Hal Leonard Online at **www.halleonard.com**

Prices, contents, and availability subject to change without notice.
Some products may not be available outside the U.S.A.